391

Special clothes

CONTENTS

D0682321

Wearing special clothes

Do you ever have to wear special clothes?

When you dress up in different clothes
you feel like a different person.

Actors wear special clothes when they act in plays. Actors' clothes are called costumes.

Clothes for sport

T-shirt

shorts

You need clothes that are easy to move in for some sports.

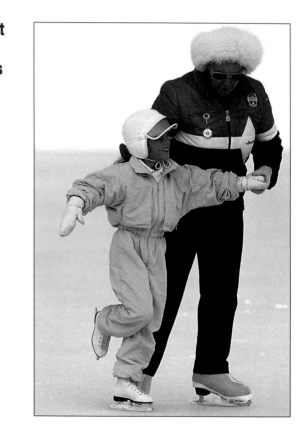

It's fun to wear the same strip as your favourite team.

Sometimes everyone in a team wears clothes that are the same colour.

You need clothes that protect you for some sports.

helmet

shoulder pads

knee pads

life-jacket

Sometimes you must wear a life-jacket.

Clothes for dancing

You need different clothes for different kinds of dancing.

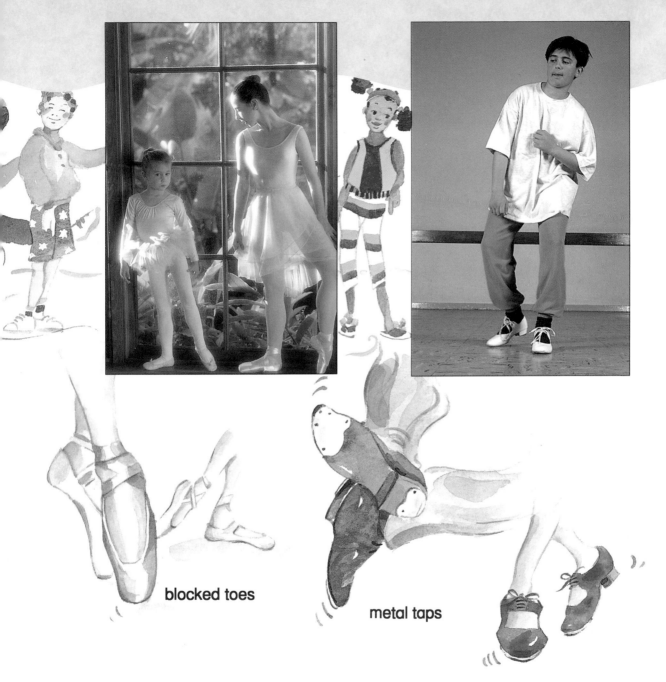

blocked toes

metal taps

A dancer's shoes are very important.

Clothes for weddings

Everyone wears their best clothes at a wedding.

Sometimes the family of the bride or groom wear clothes that are the same colour.

yellow turbans

A bride always wears special clothes. They may be red, white, yellow or another colour. The groom wears special clothes too.

veil

Clothes for festivals

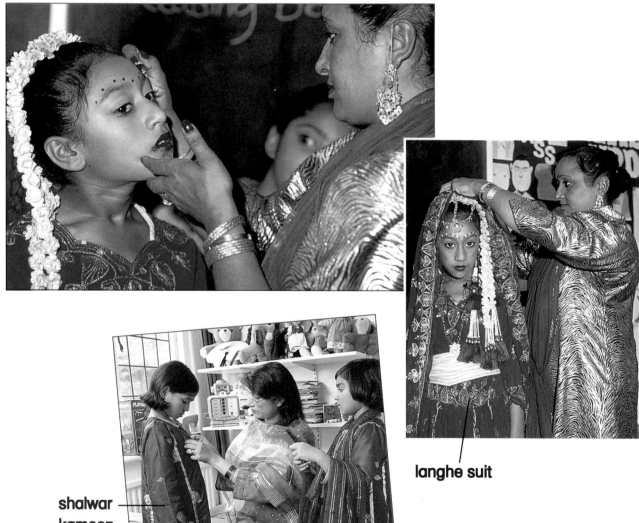

langhe suit

shalwar kameez

People wear special clothes for festivals.

There is a parade for the Chinese New Year Festival. People dress up in dragon costumes.

Everyone comes to watch.

People wear splendid costumes at Carnival.

The costumes take weeks to make.

Index